Dinosaur World

Claire Llewellyn and
Thea Feldman

KINGFISHER
NEW YORK

KINGFISHER
LONDON & NEW YORK

Copyright © Kingfisher 2012
Published in the United States by Kingfisher,
175 Fifth Ave., New York, NY 10010
Kingfisher is an imprint of Macmillan Children's Books, London.
All rights reserved.

Distributed in the U.S. and Canada by Macmillan,
175 Fifth Ave., New York, NY 10010

Library of Congress Cataloging-in-Publication data
has been applied for.

Series editor: Thea Feldman
Literacy consultant: Ellie Costa, Bank St. College, New York

ISBN: 978-0-7534-6760-2 (HB)
ISBN: 978-0-7534-6761-9 (PB)

Kingfisher books are available for special promotions
and premiums. For details contact: Special Markets
Department, Macmillan, 175 Fifth Ave., New York, NY 10010.

For more information, please visit
www.kingfisherbooks.com

Printed in China
9 8 7 6 5 4 3 2 1
1TR/0211/WKT/UNTD/115MA

Picture credits
The Publisher would like to thank the following for permission to reproduce their material. Every care has
been taken to trace copyright holders. However, if there have been unintentional omissions or failure to trace
copyright holders, we apologize and will, if informed, endeavor to make corrections in any future edition.
Top = t; Bottom = b; Center = c; Left = l; Right = r
Pages 11 Shutterstock/Amy Johansson; 28 Frank Lane Picture Agency/ Mark Newman;
29t Shutterstock/mikeledray; 29b Shutterstock/vaida; all other images from the Kingfisher Artbank.

Contents

Welcome to Dinosaur World!

Have you ever been to a wildlife park?
The animals move around freely. You
watch them from the safety of a car or bus.
You can see up close how animals live.

Dinosaur

This way to
the dinosaurs

Now imagine a dinosaur park like that.
In Dinosaur World, dinosaurs are alive!
You can ride a tour bus to see them up close.

What are you waiting for? Let's go!

Who is in the park?

Take a look at this map. It shows the park and which dinosaurs live in it.

Be sure to stay on the bus at all times. Every dinosaur has a danger rating.

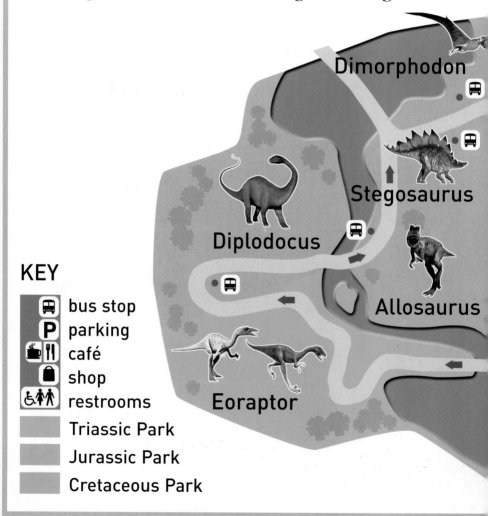

Dimorphodon

Stegosaurus

Diplodocus

Allosaurus

Eoraptor

KEY

🚌	bus stop
🅿	parking
☕🍴	café
🔒	shop
♿🚻	restrooms
	Triassic Park
	Jurassic Park
	Cretaceous Park

Even plant eaters are dangerous. You will see how big and strong they are. So keep your head and arms inside the bus too!

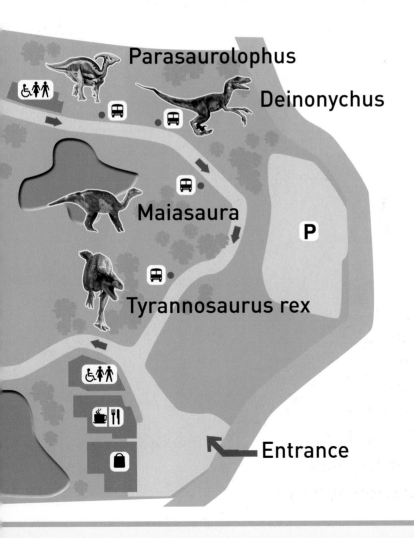

Parasaurolophus

Deinonychus

Maiasaura

P

Tyrannosaurus rex

Entrance

Step back in time

Dinosaurs were animals that really lived on Earth. They lived millions of years ago during three different time periods, or **eras**. The eras were called the Triassic, the Jurassic, and the Cretaceous.

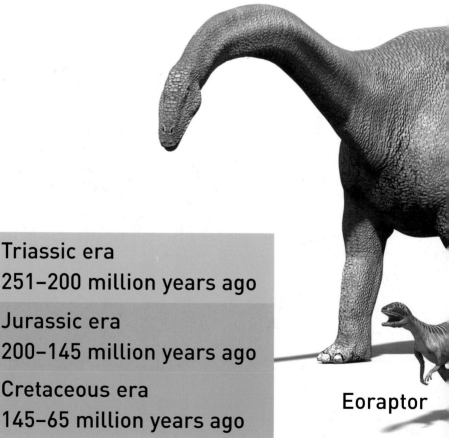

Triassic era
251–200 million years ago

Jurassic era
200–145 million years ago

Cretaceous era
145–65 million years ago

Eoraptor

Dinosaurs were the most important animals in all three eras. Today's bus tour will take you to two eras. These two eras were the busiest time for dinosaurs!

Dinosaurs come in many shapes and sizes.

Diplodocus

Deinonychus

Stegosaurus

First stop: Diplodocus

Diplodocus is huge! It has a big body, strong legs, a long neck, a small head, and a long tail. Diplodocus eats bushes and trees.

An animal this big that eats plants has to eat a lot. It spends the day tearing leaves with its teeth. Plants are hard to digest. So Diplodocus swallows stones. The stones in its stomach help grind up the plants!

Diplodocus has teeth like this.

Diplodocus eats a lot of **ferns** every day.

Fact sheet: Diplodocus
Size: up to 115 feet (35 meters) long
Habitat: near rivers
Food: ferns, moss, bushes, tree leaves
Lived: 155–145 million years ago,
   during the Jurassic era
Danger rating:

Next stop: Allosaurus

You might want to close your eyes. Allosaurus is one of the deadliest killers of its time. What makes it such a good hunter?

Allosaurus can spot animals that are sick or weak. It also runs very fast on its strong back legs. And it has big jaws, sharp teeth, and long claws to strip flesh from its **prey**.

Fact sheet: Allosaurus
Size: up to 30 feet (9 meters) long
Habitat: grasslands and forests
Food: meat
Lived: 155–144 million years ago, during the Jurassic era

Danger rating: ★ ★ ★

Stegosaurus

Stegosaurus is about the same size as Allosaurus. But Stegosaurus walks on four legs. It has hard **plates** along its back and **spines** on its tail.

The plates make it hard for a meat eater to attack. If a meat eater does attack, Stegosaurus swings its tail. It slashes the meat eater with its spines!

Stegosaurus has sharp spines on its tail.

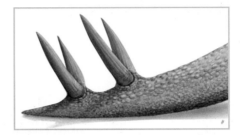

Fact sheet: Stegosaurus
Size: about 30 feet (9 meters) long
Habitat: woods
Food: moss, ferns, **conifers**
Lived: 156–140 million years ago, during the Jurassic era

Danger rating: ★ ☆ ☆

Dimorphodon

Look up! Dimorphodon is flying in the sky. It is an animal called a **pterosaur**. It looks a lot like a bird. But it is not like any bird you know today.

Look closer. Birds have no teeth. Dimorphodon has jaws full of teeth. Birds have feathers on their wings. Dimorphodon has wings covered in skin.

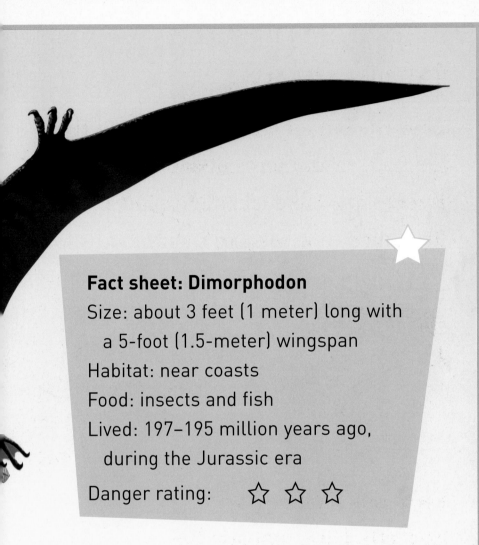

Fact sheet: Dimorphodon

Size: about 3 feet (1 meter) long with a 5-foot (1.5-meter) wingspan

Habitat: near coasts

Food: insects and fish

Lived: 197–195 million years ago, during the Jurassic era

Danger rating: ☆ ☆ ☆

Dimorphodon has lots of sharp teeth in its jaws.

Duckbill dinosaurs

Now the bus enters the Cretaceous era. Do you see the herds of dinosaurs by the river? They are duckbill dinosaurs. They are called that because their mouths look a lot like duck beaks.

Parasaurolophus

There are different kinds of duckbill dinosaurs. Each kind has a different crest on its head and a different skin pattern too. Some duckbills honk or squeak, while others make loud calls. Parasaurolophus has a loud, booming call.

Crests come in different colors and shapes.

Fact sheet: Parasaurolophus
Size: about 33 feet (10 meters) long
Habitat: rivers, lakes, coasts
Food: pine needles, leaves, twigs, ferns
Lived: 76–65 million years ago, during the Cretaceous era

Danger rating:  ★ ☆ ☆

Deinonychus

Deinonychus is the size of a small car! It has long, slim legs and runs very fast. It has 60 curving teeth in its mouth. It has sharp claws on its hands and feet. One claw on each foot is about 5 inches (13 centimeters) long and curved to cut prey.

Deinonychus hunts in **packs** and eats whatever it can find. A pack can kill a big duckbill and other large plant eaters.

Fact sheet: Deinonychus

Size: up to 10 feet (3 meters) long

Habitat: swamps and forests

Food: meat

Lived: 115–108 million years ago, during the Cretaceous era

Danger rating: ★ ★ ★

Look at the long claw!

A Deinonychus pack attacks a large plant eater.

Maiasaura

Some Maiasaura duckbill dinosaurs are nesting in the sand by a lake. Do you see the sneaky little dinosaur with an egg in its jaws? That is a Chirostenotes.

A baby Maiasaura is very small when it hatches. The herd waits for the babies to grow bigger. Then they leave to look for food. The herd will be back the next year to nest again.

A Maiasaura egg

Fact sheet: Maiasaura
Size: about 30 feet (9 meters) long
Habitat: by rivers and lakes
Food: leaves, berries, seeds, ferns, conifers
Lived: 80–65 million years ago, during the Cretaceous era
Danger rating (nesting):

Tyrannosaurus rex

Tyrannosaurus rex is one of the biggest hunters of the Cretaceous era. Its massive head has jaws strong enough to cut bone.

Tyrannosaurus rex hunts alone. It creeps up close to a plant eater. Then it charges on its strong back legs. It grabs the animal in its jaws, then bites it with its teeth. Its teeth are as long and sharp as daggers. If a tooth breaks, a new one grows in its place.

Fact sheet: Tyrannosaurus rex
Size: about 40 feet (12 meters) long
Habitat: warm forests, near
   rivers and swamps
Food: meat
Lived: 85–65 million years ago,
   during the Cretaceous era
Danger rating:

Some Tyrannosaurus teeth are 1 foot (30 centimeters) long.

End of the line

And that is the end of the tour.
Dinosaurs became **extinct** about
65 million years ago. Scientists are
still learning a lot about them. They
study **fossils** they dig out of rocks.

These people are digging out
the fossils of dinosaur bones.

How a fossil is made

A dinosaur dies. Sand and mud cover its **remains**.

The sand and mud protect the remains from wind and weather. The remains become fossils.

The sand and mud become rock. Experts go on a dinosaur dig and dig fossils out of the rock.

You can see dinosaurs

You cannot really go to Dinosaur World. But you can go to a museum that exhibits dinosaur fossils. Sometimes there are enough fossils to make a whole skeleton of a dinosaur!

A Tyrannosaurus rex skeleton in the American Museum of Natural History

Not all fossils are bones. Some are footprints. They show how an animal stood and moved. They can show if it lived alone or in a herd. Fossils of all kinds help us learn about the long ago world of dinosaurs.

A fossilized dinosaur footprint

You can see the bony plates along the back of this Stegosaurus skeleton.

Glossary

conifers trees that grow cones, such as pine trees

eras periods of time in the past

extinct a kind of animal or plant that no longer exists

ferns types of flowerless plants

fossils parts of animals that have turned to stone

packs groups of animals that hunt together

plates hard bones that protect an animal's body

prey an animal hunted for food

pterosaur a flying animal that lived in the Jurassic era

remains what is left of a living thing after it dies

spines sharp, pointed bones

Dinosaur names

The dinosaurs and other animals in this book have long names. This is how you say them.

Allosaurus: al-oh-SAW-russ

Chirostenotes: kie-roh-sten-OH-teez

Deinonychus: die-NON-i-kuss

Dimorphodon: die-MORF-oh-don

Diplodocus: di-PLOD-oh-kuss

Eoraptor: EE-oh-rap-tor

Maiasaura: my-ah-SAW-rah

Parasaurolophus: par-ah-saw-ROH-loaf-us

pterosaur: TERR-oh-sawr

Stegosaurus: steg-oh-SAW-russ

Tyrannosaurus rex: tie-RAN-oh-saw-russ rex

Index